A New Country

by Ángela Blanco

PEARSON

Glenview, Illinois • Boston, Massachusetts • Chandler, Arizona
Upper Saddle River, New Jersey

New York City

Cartagena

Cartagena, a city in Colombia

My name is Ángela. A year ago, my family came to the United States. We moved from Cartagena, Colombia, to New York City.

We moved because my father got a job in New York City. He is a doctor.

I was excited! I like to do new things and meet new people.

Moving here was easy for my parents. They had visited New York many times. They speak English very well. They studied in the United States for many years.

New York City

But moving to the United States has not been so easy for me. I thought I knew English. I was wrong!

At the airport in New York City, I was surprised. Everyone spoke so quickly! It was hard for me to understand them. And when I spoke, people could not always understand me.

John F. Kennedy airport in New York City

A house in Cartagena, Colombia

There were other differences. In Cartagena we lived in a house. We had a garden with lemon trees. In New York, we live in an apartment. We have no garden.

But then I made friends with Luisa. She lives in our building. Luisa is from Mexico. She speaks Spanish and English.

A Colombian family

Luisa helped me understand many things. "Many people here do not visit their families often," she said. "It is different in Colombia and Mexico."

Sometimes I am homesick. I miss my relatives in Colombia. I saw them all the time. We had parties and big meals together.

---

relatives: family members such as grandparents, aunts, uncles, and cousins

Luisa described other differences. "In Mexico, we greet people with a kiss on the cheek. Not here! Here you smile and say, 'Hi.'"

I said, "In Colombia, it is polite to leave some food on your plate at a meal."

"But here," Luisa said, "it is polite to eat *everything* on your plate."

A kiss on the cheek

---

polite: good manners

Best friends

It is hard to learn what to do in a new country. So many things are different! How can you learn what to do? I can tell you. Find a friend like Luisa. Luisa is a great teacher. We are also best friends.